Master Thomas Aquinas
and the Fullness of Life

The University of Dallas Aquinas Lectures
are published in cooperation with
St. Augustine's Press.

Master Thomas Aquinas and the Fullness of Life

John F. Boyle

Foreword by Philipp W. Rosemann

ST. AUGUSTINE'S PRESS
South Bend, Indiana

Manufactured in the United States of America

1 2 3 4 5 6   20 19 18 17 16 15 14

Library of Congress Cataloging in Publication Data
Boyle, John F., 1958–
Master Thomas Aquinas and the fullness of life /
John F. Boyle; foreword by Philipp W. Rosemann.
– 1st [edition].
pages cm
Includes bibliographical references.
ISBN 978-1-58731-493-3 (clothbound: alk. paper)
1. Thomas, Aquinas, Saint, 1225?-1274. I. Title.
B765.T54B66 2014
230'.2092 – dc23   2014000923

∞ The paper used in this publication meets the minimum
requirements of the American National Standard for
Information Sciences Permanence of Paper for Printed
Materials, ANSI Z39.481984.

ST. AUGUSTINE'S PRESS
www.staugustine.net

Contents

Foreword

The Philosophy Department of the University of Dallas has hosted an annual Aquinas Lecture since 1982, usually on or around January 28, St. Thomas's feast day. In the spirit of St. Thomas himself, the goal of the lecture series is to develop contemporary Catholic thought in close dialogue with the tradition—above all, of course, with Aquinas's own work. The speakers invited have covered a broad spectrum of Thomism. Some have set out to present a particularly important or intriguing area of Thomas's thought, and explain it to the audience. Others have attempted to defend Thomas's teachings against contemporary challenges, or have endeavored to develop Thomism in more of a give and take with current ideas. One important feature of the Aquinas Lecture has to do with the events surrounding it: the Aquinas Lecturer is usually invited to stay on campus for a few days, teach a seminar on a text of his or her choice, share meals with faculty, and meet informally with students. This creates the opportunity for the community not just to listen to the lecture, but also to engage in a genuine exchange with the lecturer. The Aquinas Lecture and most of the events associated with it are open to the general public.

The list of Aquinas Lecturers who have addressed the university community over the past thirty years is long and impressive. The most eminent Thomists, whether in a broader or narrower sense of the term, have all spoken on our campus: Norris Clark, Ralph McInerny, Alasdair MacIntyre, John Haldane, Robert George, Eleonore Stump, Jan Aertsen, Jean-Luc Marion, John Milbank, and Alain de Libera are just a few of the well-known colleagues whom we have had the honor to receive, and who have been awarded our Aquinas Medal.

The caliber of our speakers, and the interest of their work, quickly made it appear desirable to render their lectures accessible to a wider audience. When the University of Dallas housed the editorial offices of the *American Catholic Philosophical Quarterly*, the Aquinas Lecturer was given the opportunity to publish his or her lecture in the *ACPQ*. Beginning in 2013, the Aquinas Lectures will appear in a series of small books, which St. Augustine's Press of South Bend, Ind., has agreed to publish. Our warmest thanks are here expressed to Mr. Bruce Fingerhut for taking on this project, in particular at a time when the publishing of traditional books—traditional in content as well as form—is no longer something that can be taken for granted. Each of the little books will comprise around 100 pages, which means that the Aquinas Lecturer will be afforded an opportunity to expand upon the material presented in the one-hour lecture. We are hoping that the lectures will be composed and presented in a style accessible not just to experts, but to students and the general educated public. We have in mind a style in the mode of a C. S. Lewis or a Josef Pieper: at once learned and graceful, and not encumbered with excessive technicalities.

The Philosophy Department of the University of Dallas is delighted that Professor John F. Boyle, of the University of St. Thomas in St. Paul, Minnesota, is the first of our Aquinas Lecturers to see his lecture published in this new format.

Professor Boyle's lecture is a piece that combines a profoundly personal element—the experience of someone who has chosen St. Thomas as his own teacher and master—with the learnedness of one of the most respected contemporary American scholars of the thought of Thomas Aquinas. What we are offered in Professor Boyle's lecture is not the kind of arid and lifeless speculation that is sometimes—albeit mistaken-ly—associated with Aquinas's own style. Boyle emphasizes that Aquinas was far from being a "brain on a stick," a theologian and thinker so deeply immersed in speculation as to lose sight of the real world, and indeed of what matters in the real world. For what matters in the real world is life, and our ability to conduct this life in a way that is in accordance with the deepest longings of human nature. Boyle demonstrates, with both learning and wit, that it is precisely this life, in its fullness, to which St. Thomas endeavors to lead his students through his teaching. This life has its roots in the humble operations of living that we share with creatures such as plants and animals; it rises to the properly human level in the self-direction of which we are capable through intel-lect and will, and which enables us to form ourselves morally in habits that become "second natures" for us; and it is perfected in the supernatural life of faith in which Christ becomes our teacher and master, who leads us to eternal life with his Father.

With Master Boyle through Master Thomas to *the* Master: that could be the motto of this Aquinas Lecture. May it be the first in a long series that will help many to think, catholically and Thomistically, about what it means to live a meaningful life in the contemporary world.

Philipp W. Rosemann
Chair
Department of Philosophy
University of Dallas

Acknowledgments

I wish to express my most heartfelt gratitude to Dr. Philipp Rosemann, who invited me, on behalf of the philosophy faculty of the University of Dallas, to give the 2013 Aquinas Lecture. I am honored to have been invited. The lecture was an opportunity for me to consider in explicit ways some of the connecting tissues that unify my seemingly disparate scholarly work on St. Thomas Aquinas. In this light, I can only hope the reader will forgive the excessive self-citation in the notes. At the very least this restrained me from yet greater expansion of the talk for publication; and, perhaps, they will be of some value for the reader interested in further considerations of some of the topics here addressed.

Introduction

Teachers, living or dead, can be much like friends. Some friends are friends on first meeting. A brief conversation, and one recognizes the shared interests, shared sympathies, the intangible delight in each other's company. Other friends are rather longer in the making. By good fortune, or perhaps providence, one's paths cross over time, and at some point one recognizes that this person is indeed a friend. One is not quite sure when it happened, or perhaps even how it happened, but happen it did, and one is grateful. As I say, teachers can be much like friends. There are those teachers—perhaps living in the classroom, perhaps long dead and known through their books and sometimes through living intellectual traditions—whom one recognizes as kindred intellects of shared interests and of whom one says all but immediately, This is someone from whom I can learn, from whom I want to learn. And then there are those teachers who do not, at first encounter, particularly excite or inspire, but for whatever reason one is nonetheless forced into their company over time and, at some point, one realizes, I am learning from this teacher. I like this teacher. This teacher is a master. I want this teacher to be my master. It is in this sense of "teacher" that I speak of Thomas Aquinas in my title as "master" Thomas.

My own experience of Aquinas was of the slow kind that sneaks up on one. I first read him as an undergraduate and could, in fact, make little of him. I could see that he was smart enough; I could also see that he was incomprehensible. After twenty-five years of teaching, I think I can safely say that my experience was not unusual. I have colleagues who read Thomas, and it was immediate friendship. But for many of us—students, readers, and teachers—the first experiences of Master Thomas are ones of sparse texts and technical vocabulary, in which even the words I know are not used as I use them. The prose lacks blood. This man is no Augustine. It takes but a brief encounter to think that Aquinas is simply a brain on a stick. And so I thought.

Thirty-three years ago, I found myself in

graduate school at the Pontifical Institute of Mediaeval Studies in Toronto. In those days, the Pontifical Institute was a hotbed of Thomists. Even though my own interests on arrival were of a different sort—twelfth-century speculative mystical theology—I was smart enough to know that I ought to study with the greats, even if it meant I had to read Aquinas. And so I did. Somewhere in the midst of that study, I came to realize that St. Thomas was no longer an impenetrable burden: he was a teacher; he was increasingly my teacher. He had become, if I may so speak, a friend. Precisely how this happened is still unclear to me. But happen it did, and it has shaped the way in which I have thought about and studied Thomas ever since. He is a remarkable teacher, in spite of the all too common initial reaction of revulsion and distaste on the part of readers. And so I would like to reflect on Master Thomas precisely as a master, as a teacher.

I.

Master Thomas

It is easy enough to approach Thomas in an inadequate way, a way which his style at first all but encourages. When I went to graduate school, I thought Thomas was a system to be mastered and that the way one did it was to get all the technical vocabulary down. What one needed was a good operative scholastic dictionary in one's head. Then one simply plugged in the meaning of the words as one read, and the system fell into place. If only it were so simple; and fortunately, it is not nearly so dull.

Permit me a story from my first years at the Pontifical Institute. I asked the late Fr. Leonard Boyle of the Order of Preachers (alas, no relation) if he would undertake an independent study with me of the *prima secundae* of Thomas's *Summa theologiae*, to which he graciously agreed. Early on in the semester, I came to our weekly meeting armed with a particularly thick patch of scholastic jargon. My expectation was that we would parse out the passage along the lines just indicated: spell out the definitions, put the words together, get the system. Fr. Boyle looked at the passage in question and then took off his glasses and stared silently into space. He eventually put his glasses back on and, looking at me, said simply, "Well, that's the way i'tis, isn't it?" For the task at hand, this was not a helpful answer; but it was nonetheless an exquisite answer. What Fr. Boyle had done—and he would do it time and time again—was to stop and think about the reality that Thomas was seeking to describe. The reality was the starting point; the question was how Master Thomas helps us understand that reality better. The technical language was not in the service of the master's system, it was in the service of the master's teaching: he was working to put into words what he saw in reality. This approach was not unique to Fr. Boyle; it was common enough among many of my teachers. Fr. Boyle's confrere in the Order of Preachers, Fr. James Weisheipl, taught Aristotle's *Physics* not simply as a text of historical interest, but as a text that had something true to say about the world. Who would have thought?

Thus what I thought would be a technical system, arrived at through careful study of vocabulary, proved to be something fuller. At times, Thomas's thought can strike one as messy, lacking the neatness a good system should have. I came to learn that a particularly difficult bit of Thomas often enough reflects a difficult bit of reality. Thomas does not shape reality to his system. He does not ignore the difficult or the troubling; rather, he shapes his thinking and his language in order to get reality right. This is why Thomas's writings, as capacious as they are, are not exhaustive (although we might find them exhausting). He strives for the essential, but his thought seems to be ever open to further precision and reflection. The consistent terseness and brevity of his prose are indicative of a desire not to be the last, complete, and definitive treatment of the subject. That is the aspiration of the system; such does not seem to be Thomas's aspiration. That he did not achieve it is manifest clearly enough by the rich (and at times contradictory) commentatorial traditions that claim him for their master.

In the end, I turned my attention to St. Thomas, and have kept it there for my entire professional life, for the simple reason that I think he is one of the best masters—one of the best teachers—of reality.

How does he go about teaching?

We might start with words. If I gave the impression that one ought not be concerned with definitions and the meaning of words, let me correct that now. Thomas cares deeply about such things. But arriving at a true and strict definition is a difficult business because it has to get at the very *ratio* of the thing under discussion: it has to get to the very nature of the thing precisely as it is intelligible. It is remarkably difficult for the human intellect to articulate that intelligibility of things well. For example, readers of Thomas on virtue can find themselves frustrated in trying to articulate just what he means by virtue. One cannot help but notice that Thomas has multiple descriptions of virtue. It is that which makes a man's action and the man himself good. It is also that habit by which one is disposed to perform a good action promptly, with ease, and with delight. It is a second nature. Of course, these are not mutually exclusive. They are all true of virtue. Thomas the teacher will bring each to bear as a given question requires. The careful student, at first frustrated by such a multiplicity (what does Thomas *really* mean by virtue?), comes to see that the reality itself is what matters, and that each such effort at definition and description contributes to an understanding of the thing itself in its richness and complexity. Thomas is not one to let the precisions of his thought limit or truncate the reality of things.

This is, I suppose, an instance of making distinctions. Distinctions are everywhere in Aquinas. Making distinctions is a distinctly scholastic proclivity, and Thomas is good at it. What do I mean by good at it? He makes distinctions that are actually helpful. Early in my academic life I spent time comparing Thomas with some of his second-tier contemporaries on a number of theological topics. I encountered multiple distinctions on given topics, discovering that scholastic theologians did not necessarily agree on the applicable distinctions. I encountered very complex and elaborate distinctions, but almost never at the hands of Master Thomas. His distinctions tended to be simpler and fewer than those of his contemporaries; and when he shared a distinction, he often articulated it differently. It turns out that making distinctions is a difficult business; I don't suppose I really need to tell this to students at the University of Dallas, who seem to spend so much time in intellectual conversation and debate and are inevitably, if not always explicitly, looking for the right distinction of the subject at hand or for the right way to characterize that distinction.

One of the reasons why the form of the disputed question is so useful to Thomas is that it lends itself so readily to distinctions. When one asks whether something is the case and considers both sides of the question, the answer that will be able to account for what has been said on both sides will almost inevitably, at least at the hands of Thomas, involve making distinctions with regard to the topic at hand. That one must pose a question means that one must form a proposition, and propositions give contextual precision to words. In his theological work, Thomas will sometimes ask simply whether a given proposition is true. Thomas almost always uses such questions to distinguish the meanings of the words used in the proposition so as to articulate under what understanding of the words the proposition is true and under what understanding it is false. Analyses of modes of signification and supposition are yet further instances of making distinctions.

Much of this, it seems to me, points to Thomas's keen sense of the analogical character of language. We can and do employ the same word for different things. Thomas uses the famous example from Aristotle of the word "healthy." We can speak of a healthy man, of healthy food, and of healthy urine, but we do not mean precisely the same thing in each of the three cases. The food is called "healthy" because it contributes to the health of the man; the doctor declares the urine healthy as a sign of the health of the man. And yet, that we do not have three different words to describe the health of the man, the health-causing food, and the health-signifying urine is not a deficiency of language, for the three uses of "healthy" are in fact related. It is a good thing that we use the same word across these three instances because it brings out a relationship among the three. Of course, we have work to do to see not only how the uses are related but also how they are different. We ought not to think that because we eat healthy food we should also drink healthy urine.[1]

What is the purpose of all this hard work of definition, distinction, and analogy, that is, of understanding what our words signify? We might begin where Thomas himself begins in his *Summa contra gentiles*, with the wise man.[2] The wise man is the man who establishes order; and things are best disposed, best ordered, when they are ordered fittingly according to their ends. One can be wise within a particular area of life; the wise general, for example, is wise regarding

1   These practical aspects of Thomas's teaching were brought home to me in my work editing Thomas's Roman commentary on Book I of Peter Lombard's *Book of Sentences* with Fr. Boyle, a text which provides a unique glimpse into Thomas's classroom. See Thomas Aquinas, *Lectura romana in primum Sententiarum Petri Lombardi*, ed. L. E. Boyle, O.P., and J. F. Boyle (2006). For an introduction to the work with some consideration of Thomas's classroom, see J. F. Boyle, "Aquinas' Lost *Roman Commentary*" (2012); for a fuller consideration of the teaching elements, see J. F. Boyle, "Thomas Aquinas and his *Lectura romana in primum Sententiarum Petri Lombardi*" (2010).

2   For what follows, see Thomas Aquinas, *Summa contra gentiles*, I.1.

warfare. He is able to order his troops, his supplies, the terrain, to the end of victory. Wisdom, however, in its most proper sense does not pertain to a particular area of life but to the whole of it. The name of "wise," *simpliciter*—that is, without qualification—is reserved for that man who considers the end of the whole of the universe. And because the end of the universe is also its principle and beginning, the Philosopher teaches that the wise man considers the highest causes. He orders his mind to this truth, in accord with which he orders and governs his own life.

The wise man may also be a teacher. The best teachers are wise, for they express this ordering of their minds and lives to others. The wise man expresses his wisdom precisely through words and propositions. He must order his words; he must order them to one another, to the limitations of his own mind, and to reality. In so doing, the wise man becomes a teacher, a good teacher, a master. Insofar as he is a master, words are his tools.

The task of the wise man, to order, opens up another aspect of Master Thomas's work. Things do not exist in isolation; they exist in relation, ordered one to another. That words work analogically is an expression of precisely this fundamental interrelationship of things. There is a relationship among physical well-being, food, and urine, and the word "healthy" is an expression of it. Indeed, it would seem true to say that part of understanding things rightly is to understand their interplay, their relations, or—to speak in more explicitly Thomistic terms as related to the wise man—to understand the causality of things.

The more one understands something in its causes, the more one understands the thing itself. To understand what constitutes it (the formal and material causes), to understand the external causes that brought it into being (the efficient causes), and to understand its purpose (the final cause, the cause of causes) is to grow in understanding the thing. To consider the two external causes—efficient and final—is to see that thing in relation to other things. Indeed, it is to realize that my understanding of this thing is ultimately dependent upon my understanding of other things, on an understanding of the causal order of things. In turn, in understanding a thing, I come to understand the causality it exercises, which opens up another set of relations among things.

This is what the wise teacher does in studying any given science. He seeks to understand and then articulate the fundamental causal relations in those things studied by that science. The more rightly and profoundly he sees, the wiser he becomes; the more skillfully he explains what he sees, the better a teacher he becomes. This is true in science as we now narrowly construe the word; it is also true in the expansive construal of the word in the Middle Ages.

In theology, my teacher Fr. Weisheipl argued for just such an understanding of *sacra doctrina*, that is, sacred doctrine or, more properly, sacred teaching.[3] According to Fr. Weisheipl, the teacher of sacred doctrine—that is, the theologian—does what any teacher of a science does: he articulates the causal interrelationships among the things studied in that science. In the case of *sacra doctrina*, what is being studied are revealed truths of the faith. The theologian draws out the causal connections because in so doing he brings out

3 See J. A. Weisheipl, O.P., "The Meaning of *Sacra Doctrina* in *Summa Theologiae* I, q. 1" (1974).

more clearly the very intelligibility of the things revealed, for things are better known as they are known in their causes. Thomas gives as an example St. Paul in his First Letter to the Corinthians, who teaches that because Christ has risen, so too all shall rise (see 1 Cor 15:12–22).[4] Apparently some in Corinth had doubted the universal resurrection of the dead. St. Paul argues, in his usual truncated way, that there must be a universal resurrection of the dead because Jesus Christ has risen from the dead. What Master Thomas sees in Master Paul is the articulation of the causality of the resurrection. If one truly understands the resurrection of Christ, one understands, in part at least, its causality, which includes the resurrection of the dead at the end of time. As Fr. Weisheipl pointed out, both the resurrection of Christ and the universal resurrection of the dead are revealed truths. St. Paul is not creating new truth; he is not deducing something new from revelation. He is bringing out the causal relationship between two revealed realities.

This is in a sustained way the task of a *summa*. The high Middle Ages saw *summae* in

4   ST I.1.8.resp.

different fields of study. At its best, a *summa* was a summation of a discipline according to the fundamental principles of knowing, that is, according to causality. By way of contrast, consider the alphabetical encyclopedia. These seem to be appearing in many fields of study in our own time; publishers' catalogs routinely have new encyclopedias of just about everything. Of course these can be helpful if one is looking something up. Yet the organization is entirely extrinsic to the subject matter, for it is alphabetical. No teacher worth a hill of beans would teach chemistry with an encyclopedia of chemistry as the textbook, requiring students to read it from A to Z. A medieval *summa* sought to present the whole of a field of study not according to extrinsic principles of organization (for example, alphabetically) but according to intrinsic principles of organization, that is, according to the causal relationships of things. I might note, by way of an aside, that it says something about the Middle Ages that it produced so many *summae*, while it says something about our time that it produces few *summae* and many encyclopedias.

This drive to order things that is proper to the wise man characterizes Thomas's teaching.

Although Thomists mine the *Summa theologiae* as if it were an encyclopedia—just one that requires a usable index—the fact is that it is a *summa*, which means that Thomas is out to give order to his discipline and to do so precisely along the lines of causality as found in the careful study of things—in this case, first and foremost revealed things. That there are many ways to explore something as rich as sacred doctrine can be seen in the fact that Thomas undertook four *summae* in his life: his Parisian commentary on Peter Lombard's *Book of Sentences*, the *Summa contra gentiles*, the *Summa theologiae*, and the *Compendium theologiae*. Each of these works is organized differently. Thomas does not think there is but one way to order sacred teaching. The particular and limited vantage point and intention of the theologian will give shape to the order of the material. This does not mean, of course, that all ordering is equal; the wise man orders well, and not all theologians then or now are wise.

II.

Life

An example of what I have been speaking about is in order, indeed overdue. I turn to the topic found in the second half of my title: life, or rather, the fullness of life. Forgive me for a turn of phrase— "fullness of life"—that is not Thomas's, but which nonetheless expresses what I want to explore here in Thomas's teaching. What does it mean to speak of the life of man? What does the life of man in its fullness, at its perfection, look like?

Let us begin with the first and most explicit consideration of life in the *Summa theologiae*, in which Thomas addresses what it can mean to speak of God as the living God.[1] Scripture so speaks of God, for example in Psalm 83: "my

1   ST I.18.

heart and my flesh have exulted in the living God." But how precisely are we to understand this?

The Degrees of Natural Life

Thomas begins with the word itself. What do we mean when we say something lives? What is the reality of which we speak? In common speech, we call some things "living," but not all things. We begin with a distinction in reality manifest in speech. So what distinguishes living things from non-living things? Thomas appeals to the master of the study of living things, Aristotle, and with him, he follows the common use of the word. We call those things "living" which move themselves or bring themselves to some act.[2] Since rocks do not move themselves, we do not call them "living"; dogs, on the other hand, do move themselves, so that we do call them "living." Thomas pushes further: does this mean, then, that life is some kind of operation? Is life something we do? It would seem that it is, since living is something we do. Thomas here may surprise. While it is

2   ST I.18.1.resp.

true that because something moves itself we say
it lives, the word "life" does not actually signify
that movement or those operations; rather, it signifies the substance which, according to its
nature, moves itself or performs some operation
by itself. "To live is nothing other than to be in
such a nature."[3] The operations of life follow
from the very being of the thing, which is to live.
Thus, when one lives, one is in fact doing something, but what one is doing is being, antecedent
to any particular operations of a living thing.

With this description of life in place, Thomas is
ready to address the specific question of whether it
is fittingly attributed to God.[4] He answers simply
that life is most especially and properly in God. To
explain this idea, Thomas looks to the *ratio* of life,
self-movement. The more perfectly self-moving
something is, the more perfectly does it live. Our

3   ST I.18.2.resp.: "vivere nihil aliud est quam esse in
     tali natura." In the sed contra, Thomas quotes
     Aristotle: "For living things, to live is to be" [*Sed
     contra est quod dicit Philosophus in II de Anima:
     "vivere viventibus est esse"*]. He confirms his point
     in the response by saying that "living" is not an acci-
     dental but substantial predicate.
4   ST I.18.3.resp.

common speech already recognizes kinds and degrees of living things when we speak of plants, animals, and human beings. But what does "more perfectly self-moving" mean? Here we push more deeply into the reality of living things. Thomas turns to a threefold order found more broadly in all moving things:

> First, the end moves the agent; but the principal agent is that which acts through its own form; and it sometimes acts through some instrument, which does not act from the power of its own form but from the power of the principal agent; to this instrument only the execution of the action pertains.[5]

Thomas sees how the threefold order speculatively articulated according to end, form, and instru-

---

5   ST I.18.3.resp.: "In moventibus autem et motis tria per ordinem inveniuntur. Nam primo, finis movet agentem; agens vero principale est quod per suam formam agit; et hoc interdum agit per aliquod instrumentum, quod non agit ex virtutibus suae formae, sed ex virtute principalis agentis; cui instrumento competit sola executio actionis."

ment found in all moving things can be applied to living things commonly distinguished as plants, animals, and human beings. In evaluating living things, we face the question as to the degree to which the living thing is self-moving. It need not have each grade or degree, but the more perfect kind of self-moving being will be self-moving with respect to all three: end, form, and instrument. The three grades of living things in the natural order—plants, animals, and human beings— follow the threefold order in reverse from less to more perfectly self-moving.

Thomas is very careful and precise here because another distinction stands in the background. Nature is a principle of motion and rest for all natural things. Now natural beings, precisely as natural, have a form and an end given them by nature according to which they are moved. This is true even of elements, fire and water for example, which have form and end according to which fire moves upward and water downward. We do not, however, call such things "living," in spite of their natural motion, except perhaps by way of similitude.[6] Thus, for

---

6 See ST I.18.1.ad 2m and ad 3m.

natural things that are living there is need for something more, and that is a self-movement proper to their nature with regard to end, form, or instrument.

(1) First and least perfect are plants, which move themselves in a very limited way; they take nutrition, grow, and some put out, more or less, leaves, flowers, and fruit. Plants have an end determined by nature. Plants also have a form from nature, which is determined and not itself acted upon. There is, in short, no movement within the plant by which one could speak of self-movement with regard to either the form or the end, which are entirely determined by nature. The self-moving of the plant—its taking nutrition and its growth—are actions of the form but executed by the material organs of the plant, which are moved as instruments by the form according to the end. For plants then, there is no true self-movement with regard to either end or form, but only with regard to instrumental execution of actions.[7]

7 ST I.18.3.resp.: "Invenientur igitur quaedam, quae movent seipsa, non habito respectu ad formam vel finem, quae inest eis a natura, sed solum quantum ad executionem motus; sed forma per quam agunt, et

(2) Next are animals. Animals also move themselves according to the execution of actions, that is, according to the instrumentality of bodily organs and parts. But there is something higher in the case of animals. Animals have senses through which they apprehend the forms of other things. These forms, apprehended through sense, are principal agents for the self-movement of animals. The sophistication of the sensation determines the perfection of this kind of self-moving. Oysters have only touch, opening and closing as a result of what they perceive through touch. Dogs have fuller sense powers, so that they are able to move themselves locally with regard to things perceived at a distance. Animals are

finis propter quem agunt, determinantur eis a natura. Et huiusmodi sunt plantae, quae secundum formam inditam eis a natura, movent seipsas secundum augmentum et decrementum." I take *habito* here (and it will recur at parallel points with regard to animals and man in this response) as that species of immediate ordered consequence following from a principle that Aristotle discusses in his *Physics*, for which Thomas's commentary is most helpful; see Thomas Aquinas, *In octo libros Physicorum Aristotelis expositio*, Book V, lectio 5, esp. no. 689.

moved as an immediate consequence of the act of the principal agent, the form received through the senses. It is proper to the nature of an animal to receive such forms through their senses; such forms received act upon the soul receiving them. The animal is moved as a result of the form received through the senses. It is moved, first, in immediate consequence of the act of the form received through the senses; secondly, in its own form, the soul; and, thirdly, in whatever parts of the body by way of consequent actions mediated by organs and limbs. There is thus self-movement because the animal, through its senses, receives the forms which are the principles of these kinds of self-movement. Because these forms are received by the soul, the motions that follow are beyond those determined simply and directly by the form of the animal as given by nature, for the latter are necessary and natural but cannot qualify as self-movement.

What remains entirely determined in the animal is the end. The animal does not establish the end of its actions prior to them. With regard to its natural end, it is moved simply by instinct. Thus, while there is self-movement in the animal with regard to form, there is none with regard to end.[8]

(3) Finally, there is man. In man there is self-movement by way of instrumental execution of the action, and there is also self-movement immediately consequent upon form received through the senses. In addition, however, there is self-movement that is immediately consequent upon

---

8   ST I. 18.3.resp.: "Quaedam vero ulterius movent seipsa, non solum habito respectu ad executionem motus, sed etiam quantum ad formam quae est principium motus, quam per se acquirunt. Et huiusmodi sunt animalia, quorum motus principium est forma non a natura indita, sed per sensum accepta. Unde quanto perfectiorem sensum habent, tanto perfectius movent seipsa. Nam ea quae non habent nisi sensum tactus, movent ut solum infra seipsa motu dilationis et constrictionis, ut ostrea, parum excedentia motum plantae. Quae vero habent virtutem sensitivam perfectam, non solum ad cognoscendum coniuncta et tangentia, sed etiam ad cognoscendum distantia, movent seipsa in remotum motu processivo.

Sed quamvis huiusmodi animalia formam quae est principium motus, per sensum accipiant, non tamen per seipsa praestituunt sibi finem suae operationis, vel sui motus; sed est eis inditus a natura, cuius instinctu ad aliquid agendum moventur per formam sensu apprehensam."

an end not simply given in nature. The human being has the capacity to determine in advance an end upon which his action follows. That end so determined moves the man, who in turn moves himself. This requires intellect and reason, for it requires the capacity to know the proportion between an end and the means to that end and, with that, the capacity to order one thing to another. Man's intellectual nature gives him this final and highest degree of self-motion with regard to the end. In antecedently determining an end man moves himself to that end. He has the capacity to accomplish this by nature, but the actual determination of the end and the consequent self-movement are not simply the determined movement of nature. The result is that man has the complete threefold ordering of motion as self-movement: "in one and the same man the intellective power moves the sensitive powers, and the sensitive powers through their own command move the organs, which in turn execute the motion." In the case of humans, then, there is self-movement from final cause to the instrumental execution of the action.[9]

---

9   ST I.18.3.resp.: "Unde supra talia animalia sunt illa quae movent seipsa, etiam habito respectu ad finem,

There are nonetheless limitations to man's self-moving, for some aspects of that movement are determined by nature. These are the first principles, which have a determined relation to man and his intellection, and the final end, which man cannot not will. Thus it is that in some regards man moves himself, whereas in others he is necessarily moved by another according to nature.[10]

With this understanding of what it means to live for created things, Master Thomas can explain how life is fitting to God. Given what he has said, there could indeed be something yet

quem sibi praestituunt. Quod quidem non fit nisi per rationem et intellectum, cuius est cognoscere proportionem finis et eius quod est ad finem, et unum ordinare in alterum. Unde perfectior modus vivendi est eorum quae habent intellectum; haec enim perfectius movent seipsa. Et huius est signum, quod in uno et eodem homine virtus intellectiva movet potentias sensitivas; et potentiae sensitivae per suum imperium movent organa, quae exequuntur motum."

10   ST I.18.3.resp.: "Sed quamvis intellectus noster ad aliqua se agat, tamen aliqua sunt ei praestituta a natura; sicut sunt prima principia, circa quae non potest aliter se habere, et ultimus finis, quem non potest non velle."

more perfectly self-moving, and thus yet more perfectly living. What would such an entity look like? It would be a being whose nature is its very act of understanding, such that no external first principles govern its intellect, which simply is its nature. Such would be perfect self-motion with regard to form. Secondly, it would be a being that is its own end. No other thing would determine its end; it would have no action ordered to any end other than itself. Such would be perfect self-motion with regard to the end. This, Thomas says, is God. He concludes with Aristotle, who, having shown that God is understanding, maintains that God has a most perfect and simple life because his intellect is most perfect and always in act.[11]

11 ST I.18.3.resp.: "Unde, licet quantum ad aliquid moveat se, tamen oportet quod quantum ad aliqua ab alio moveatur. Illud igitur cuius sua natura est ipsum eius intelligere, et cui id quod naturaliter habet, non determinatur ab alio, hoc est quod obtinet summum gradum vitae. Tale autem est Deus. Unde in Deo maxime est vita. Unde Philosophus in XII Metaph., ostenso quod Deus sit intelligens, concludit quod habeat vitam perfectissimam et sempiternam, quia intellectus eius est perfectissimus et semper in actu."

Of course, I have dropped us well into the consideration of divine attributes of the first part of the *Summa*. Now, in accord with the principles of the wise man and the good teacher, the *Summa* is carefully ordered. Thomas has already shown that God is perfect, and that among his perfections is his understanding. Indeed, he has shown that God simply *is* his understanding.[12] Thus, he may now apply this insight to the divine life, precisely with regard to the highest mark of self-motion, the intellect. In this manner, God is rationally posited as living, and indeed living to the highest degree.

In all of this we see Thomas the Master. He considers first what we mean by the word "life" in common speech. This brings him to a distinction in reality between living and non-living things. Our speech, in turn, distinguishes among living things, plants, animals, and human beings. The subsequent distinctions of kinds of motion and degrees of living things are finely articulated from the created order. These distinctions are matters of a careful ordering that reflects the causality of self-motion. If he can help his reader

12   ST I.14.4.

understand the causal realities at the heart of the degrees of living things, he enables his reader to grasp more profoundly just what constitutes the self-motion of a living thing. Articulating the principles of form and end permits Thomas to bring the consideration of life to its ultimate perfection in God.

Also present is analogy. We see this most exquisitely in the movement of Thomas's thought from the created order to God. Thomas shows beautifully how one can understand not only that God is living, but that he possesses life most perfectly. At the same time, he has clearly taken us beyond the created order. For that perfection of life requires a being of an entirely different nature, whose being *is* his intellection, and who is himself his end. We can see that this would be a perfectly self-moved being, but we in fact no longer see the being itself. This is an essential feature of analogy with regard to God: that we understand something of God that we can truly speak, while in so doing we discover something of God that is necessarily shrouded in mystery, for it lies beyond our experience of the created order. This is why Thomas must be so attentive to the primary natural analogs in the analogy. It is these realities we know best, given the conditions of human knowing. The more clearly we articulate and express them, the more rightly can we speak and think analogically about God. If Thomas does not develop the philosophical elements at great length in the *Summa theologiae*, he has good reason: he presumes his beginners in theology have already completed their studies in philosophy. He reminds them of what they know (or at least should know). But it is good to remind them, because to speak of God as living makes sense only in relation to the natural analogs in the created order. Notably, Thomas attributes to Aristotle the analogical analysis of life from creature to God. The Christian has no doubt that God is the living God, but Aristotle helps him understand just what that might mean and, in so doing, exposes an exquisite line of perfection among things.[13]

13 This kind of analogical analysis is ubiquitous in Thomas's thought both philosophical and theological. My interest here is in Thomas's actual use of analogy as a teacher. I have considered some other instances in "St. Thomas Aquinas and the Analogy of *potentia generandi*" (2000) and "The Analogy of 'Homo' and 'Deus' in St. Thomas Aquinas's *Lectura*

The Moral Life

We find in speech still another meaning of the word "life" with regard to man. In this meaning, it is used by way of a kind of similitude. While in man there are natural principles of certain works of life according to his natural powers, there are also additional principles—namely, habits—that incline him to certain kinds of acts as if by way of nature, a kind of second nature, for they make those acts so very delightful:

> And from this it is said, as if by a kind of similitude, that that operation which is delightful to man, and to which he is inclined, and in which he conducts his life, and indeed to which he orders his life, is called the life of

romana" (2008). The much vexed contemporary question of how Thomas understood the speculative foundations of analogy is not my concern here; however, the commentatorial tradition that gives primacy to analogy of proper proportionality seems to me to sustain most fully the practical analogical work of Thomas. For a spirited articulation and defense of the analogy of proper proportionality, see S. A. Long, *Analogia entis* (2011).

man; hence some are said to live a life
of luxury, some a life of honesty.[14]

In this way we speak of a good life, an honest
life, or a dissolute life, and in so doing point to
something that is analogous to life as the very
substance of the human being. A life of virtue (or
vice) is such that those habits, those virtues (or
vices), in the acts that follow from them, come to
give shape and substance to the way a life is
lived, in the likeness of the natural powers of life
in man. To live is to be in a nature that has the
power to move itself. Man is able to give order
to that way of being so as to specify the life he
lives through habitual dispositions tending to
good (or evil). This follows from his intellect and
reason, by which he is able to establish an end
and order his actions to it. Insofar as he rightly
and habitually orders his life to the good, he is
increasingly virtuous and, as such, increasingly
delights in the life he leads. The virtues arise
from his self-motion and, when formed, in turn
so contribute to his self-motion as to be called a
kind of second nature. By means of the virtues, a

14   ST I.18.2.ad 2m.

man so orders the whole of his existence that it can be called a life, a good life. This ordering is properly the work of the wise man. Wisdom is, in short, a way of living, it is life.

Thomas concludes this consideration of "the works of life by way of a kind of similitude" with this statement: "And in this way, to know God is called eternal life."[15] To know God is not simply a matter of having learned something; it is to live. It is to be in a nature with a power habituated to the knowing of God and, so habituated, exercised with delight. Because knowing God belongs, by way of similitude, to the works of life, man can fittingly be raised to this life and be perfected by grace.[16] To know God is not simply life, it is eternal life.

The perfection of eternal life is, for Thomas, the beatific vision.[17] It is a seeing which, at least in the beatific vision, is a knowing. In that

15 ST I.18.2.ad 2m.
16 The vexed but important issues surrounding man's nature and the supernatural order of grace run through much of this lecture. A corrective to whatever infelicitous failures in precision remain in my prose is found in S. A. Long, *Natura pura* (2010).
17 ST I-II.3.8.

knowing, the intellect will be brought to its perfection, that is to say, entirely into act. Beatitude is an operation,[18] an operation of created living things at their highest and fullest: knowing to the perfection of being, such that the potency to know is fully actualized. What object, when known, can bring man to such perfection of action? Not individual truths collected—not the reading of an encyclopedia—but truth itself, that truth to which all things point as their efficient and final cause: God. This truth, however, lies beyond God simply as a cause deduced from things; it is God in his essence. It consists in seeing him, as the Apostle Paul says, face to face, which Master Thomas understands as knowing God without the mediation of created things.[19] This knowing exceeds the natural powers of the human being; only the aid of God's grace brings the soul to that end. And in so doing, it brings it not only to the essence of the divine nature of the one God, but to the three persons of Father, Son,

18 ST I-II.3.2.resp.
19 See Thomas's commentary on 1 Cor 13:12 in *Super primam epistolam ad Corinthios lectura*, chap. 13, lect. 4, in Thomas Aquinas, *Super epistolas S. Pauli lectura* (1953), vol. 1, nos. 802–03.

and Holy Spirit. As Thomas puts it succinctly at the beginning of his life as a teacher, "Knowing the Trinity in unity is the fruit and end of our entire life."[20]

In saying all this, I may not have done much to dispel the image of Master Thomas as a brain on a stick. All this discussion of the intellect is good enough, but what about the will? Where is love? Does it have any place in Master Thomas's teaching on life?

The object of love, Thomas teaches us, is the good. The good is the formal *ratio* under which the object of love is considered. That is to say, we love something, or someone, precisely insofar as that thing or person is good. In the presence of the good, we are moved towards it in a movement that belongs to the will. The good perceived draws us to itself; it is part of our self-movement, a part of our living, that we move ourselves to the good. The good to which we are ultimately drawn, however, is the knowing of God that per-

20 Thomas Aquinas, *Scriptum super libros Sententiarum*, ed. P. Mandonnet, O.P. (1929), lib. I, dist. 2, expositio textus, p. 77: "Cognitio enim Trinitatis in unitate est fructus et finis totius vitae nostrae."

fects the intellect. In the beatific vision, in seeing God face to face, this good is attained; as a consequence, the will delights in it. Such delight is the joy in truth that marks eternal life.

We can carry this reflection yet further. Revelation teaches that man is made in the image of God. Thomas follows his theological master St. Augustine in seeing this image most fully in the human soul, specifically in the acts of remembering, knowing, and loving.[21] More precisely, it is the relation among these acts that most fully constitutes the image of God in man, reflecting the dynamic operations that distinguish the divine persons. In considering the image, Thomas asks about the object of that remembering, knowing, and loving in relation to the perfection of the image. The latter is at its most perfect when it has God himself as its object: when it is God himself—Father, Son, and Holy Spirit—who is remembered, known, and loved. In this trinity of acts, the soul is most like God, who remembers, knows, and loves himself, and in whose knowing there occurs the generation of the Son and in whose loving the procession of the Holy

21 ST I.93.7.resp.

Spirit.[22] If God's life is the most perfect, man's life is most perfect in the perfection of the divine image in him.

In the actuality of the image of the triune God, one finds remembering, knowing, and loving; but one also finds a certain order since one cannot love what one does not know; furthermore, the perfection of loving is in proportion to the perfection of knowing. The order of nature here reflects the order of procession in the Trinity. In this perfection of the image in beatitude, one truly shares in the divine life. This is not a happy metaphor; this is not bad religious poetry. One shares precisely in what God's life is: his knowing and loving of himself, because in beatitude the blessed, too, know and love God as Father, Son, and Holy Spirit. Eternal life is the perfection of the will because it is the perfection of the intellect. "The knowing of the Trinity in unity is the fruit and end of our whole life."

To know God in his essence is eternal life, and its perfection is the beatific vision. But what about this side of life? Can we speak of "works of life by way of a kind of similitude" in which to

22   ST I.93.8.resp.

know God is eternal life prior to the beatific vision? Such would be possible if the human being could know his end even imperfectly in this life and then, by way of virtuous action, order his existence to it. Naturally, however, he knows God only as first cause. Any knowledge beyond this requires the theological virtues, which allow man to order his life supernaturally to God. For Thomas, such an ordering to eternal life is at the very heart of this life—we can see it in much of his teaching.

Consider the order of the *Summa theologiae*. Beatitude is the subject of the first five questions of the second part of the *Summa*. The second part—the overwhelmingly largest part of the *Summa*, so large that Thomas divided it into two further parts—is about the movement of the rational creature to God.[23] Man moves himself to his end, to his happiness; if that goal is not in place, then the progress of the movement is in doubt. Even though man does not determine his end, he can certainly determine whether and how to move to it. This matter constitutes the substance of the second part of the *Summa*, which

23   ST I.2.divisio textus.

could, in this light, be seen as Thomas's magisterial reflection on what it means for man to live in this life so as to be ordered to the fullness of life that is his final end. And what do we find in the second part? We find the totality of Thomas's treatment of man's moral and spiritual life. Moreover, we find it considered in an ordered way—again the work of the wise man—such that each element is related to the next and ultimately considered in relation to the final end. In the second part of the second part, we encounter 170 articles devoted to the virtues, theological and cardinal. Here we find Thomas on the moral life or, to use his own language, on those works of life, considered by way of a kind of similitude, proper to man by which his moral character becomes a kind of second nature.[24]

24 In his Gilson lecture of 1982 at the Pontifical Institute of Mediaeval Studies, Fr. Boyle famously situated the *Summa theologiae*—specifically the *secunda secundae*'s questions on the virtues—in the context of the thirteenth-century Dominican literature of pastoral care. See L. E. Boyle, O.P., *The Setting of the "Summa theologiae" of Saint Thomas* (1982), reprinted with revisions in L. E. Boyle, O.P., *Facing History: A Different Thomas Aquinas* (2000), 65–91.

This is another instance of Fr. Weisheipl's understanding of the order of the *Summa theologiae*. The first part treats of God, and the second of the movement of the rational creature to God. The latter is possible in its fullness only if the end is sufficiently known; hence, in the first part Thomas establishes not only the efficient cause of all things (this is why the treatment of creation is also in the first part), but also the final cause. Thomas makes this order clear in the very first article of the *Summa* on the need of a teaching—sacred teaching—beyond the disciplines known by reason: it is so man can order his life to its end of union with the revealed triune God. Thus, the *Summa* is, in its own way, Master Thomas's instruction in living wisely: to know the end and then to order one's life to that end in accord with the very moral reality of man articulated in the second part.[25]

If the perfection of human life is the beatific vision, the imperfect life here and now is to be ordered to that end. It can be more or less perfect

25 For the placement of the *tertia pars*, see J. F. Boyle, "Is the *tertia pars* of the *Summa theologiae* misplaced?" (1993–1994).

as it is more or less rightly ordered to its end. But to be rightly ordered means to know the end, and to order everything to it—that is to say, to God. For such knowledge and order to inform a life— as a second nature—requires a virtue, the theological virtue of faith. Let us consider this virtue in the context of Thomas's teachings on life.

The Supernatural Life

In the questions on faith that begin the *secunda secundae* of the *Summa theologiae*, Thomas proceeds according to the proper order for the study of a virtue: he considers first the object, then the act, and then the virtue. The object of faith is the first truth, that is, God.[26] The interior act of faith is to believe, that is, to think with assent.[27] The exterior act of faith is to confess.[28] The virtue of faith is the habitual disposition to the act of faith.[29]

And so we begin again with a consideration of a word and the reality which it signifies. In his

26 *ST* II-II.1.1.
27 *ST* II-II.2.1.
28 *ST* II-II.3.1.
29 *ST* II-II.4–7.

Letter to the Hebrews, St. Paul states, "Faith is the substance of things to be hoped for, the evidence of things that appear not" (Heb 11:1). Thomas asks whether this is a fitting definition of faith.[30] Although St. Paul's description is not in the form of a definition, it has all that is requisite for one. Thomas thus casts Paul's description in the form of a definition: "faith is a habit of the mind by which eternal life is begun in us, making the intellect assent to things that appear not."[31]

As a virtue, faith is a habit of the mind—specifically, a habit that makes the intellect assent to things that appear not. The act that follows from this habit is assent, that is, the act by which one assents to, holds firmly to, some truth. In the case of the theological virtue of faith, one assents to the truth of things that appear not. Thomas has already pointed out what this is: the first truth, that is, God. In explaining the act of faith, Thomas notes that first and foremost the act of faith consists in believing *in* a God who has revealed himself (*credere Deo*). Because one

30   ST II-II.4.1.
31   ST II-II.4.1.resp.

believes in a God who reveals, one also believes *what* he reveals (*credere Deum*).[32]

This is wholly consonant with the way in which belief works in the lives of men, quite apart from the particulars of theological faith. We all learn because, to begin with, we believe that our teachers are truth-tellers, and because of that belief, we also believe what they teach us. If we did not, we would learn very little. When Mrs. Thistlebottom tells her kindergarten class, "Boys and girls, this is the letter A," and holds up a large letter A, the students believe her. If little Johnny puts up his hand and demands of Mrs. Thistlebottom, "prove it," he may find himself standing in a corner (if they do that anymore in schools); he will certainly find himself ignorant.

In the case of the theological virtue of faith, the Christian believes in a God who reveals, and because he believes *in* him, he believes *what* he has revealed.

In analyzing the act that follows from the virtue, St. Thomas uses St. Augustine's definition of the act of faith: to think (*cogitare*) with assent.[33]

32 ST II-II.2.2.resp.
33 ST II-II.2.1.resp.

This is what human beings do: they think, and their thinking is ordered to what is true. When their thinking arrives at the truth, they assent to it; they hold firmly to it. In this case—uniquely—because the object of this act of thinking with assent is God as the first truth who cannot err, one assents with full vigor; there is no place for doubt or qualification. One assents with the same certainty with which one assents to self-evident truths.

Faith is thus a matter of the intellect. It is about knowing the truth and assenting to it. Faith is not a mere feeling; it is not a mere confidence. It is knowing the truth. Pope Benedict spoke throughout his pontificate of the modern truncation of the intellect and its attendant dangers.[34] If we consent to the modern narrowing of the

---

34 See, for example, his lecture at the meeting with representatives from the sciences at the University of Regensburg, September 12, 2006; address at the meeting with representatives from the world of culture, Collège des Bernardins, Paris, September 12, 2008; address at meeting with representatives of British society, Westminster Hall, September 17, 2010; address on a visit to the Bundestag, Berlin, September 22, 2011.

intellect, then we must find some other place for faith. Master Thomas reminds us that we simply should not accept such truncations and limitations of the intellect. The intellect is made to know the truth, and first and foremost among those truths is the first truth. We know this truth with the same intellect with which we know all truth. We assent to it with the same intellect with which we assent to all truth. I suspect that sometimes the language of faith and reason is implicitly translated into a distinction of human powers: a man reasons with his intellect, but he believes with some other mysterious faith power. Thomas reminds us with his exquisite clarity that man knows and assents to the truth with only one power, the intellect. The life of the mind is one and unified.

Precisely because of this scope and unity of the intellect, Thomas insists that what is believed can be articulated in propositions—most importantly, the articles of the creeds. This insight, too, recognizes the nature of the human intellect: man cannot fully grasp God simply as he is, nor can man grasp him even to the perfection of his own, human intellect in this life. But he can nonetheless understand some things that have been revealed and, in accord with the nature of the

human intellect, this understanding can be articulated in propositions. This does not mean that
the object of the act of faith is a proposition; the
object is the thing itself, which is expressed by the
proposition.[35] Thomas singles out the mysteries
of the Incarnation of Christ and the Trinity.[36] It
is good that these truths are articulated in the
creed, so that they can be known more easily by
all; otherwise, some might fail to know the truth
through ignorance of faith.[37] What is known is a
reality, a reality signified by and expressed in
words.

Let us return to St. Paul and Thomas. Paul
describes faith as "the substance of things to be
hoped for, the evidence of things that appear
not." Thomas recasts Paul's phrase as a definition: "a habit of mind by which eternal life is
begun in us, making the intellect assent to things
that appear not." St. Paul's "evidence of things
that appear not" corresponds to Thomas's
"assent of the intellect to things that appear not."
But what of Paul's "substance of things to be

35 ST II-II.1.2.ad 2m.
36 ST II-II.2.7 and 8.
37 ST II-II.1.9.resp.

hoped for"? This Thomas has recast as "a habit of mind by which eternal life is begun in us." One cannot help but note Thomas's introduction of life, eternal life, into the definition. How is this related to the "substance of things to be hoped for"? The object of hope is God as man's final happiness, that is, eternal life. Thomas explains that substance is sometimes called the first beginning of something, especially when the whole of that thing is contained virtually in the first principle. Faith is "the substance of things hoped for" because, in the Christian, the first beginning of things hoped for occurs through the assent of faith, which virtually contains everything to be hoped for, for he hopes to be made blessed in this, that he will see with open vision the truth to which he now adheres in faith.[38] Thus with faith, man begins eternal life here on earth. Therefore, the knowledge of God that is eternal life is not simply the beatific vision; it is also the life of faith. This is the supernatural life—"life" by way of a kind of similitude—as begun in the theological virtue of faith.

How can the Christian move himself so as to

---

38   ST II-II.4.1.resp.

live better by growing in faith? How can he grow in perfection in this singular life of knowing God? Thomas quotes Augustine to the effect that the act of faith is to think with assent. He explains that such thinking arises from the imperfection of knowledge, for it is knowledge of what is not seen.[39] One can think about what one knows in faith and come to know it more deeply. This, too, is in accord with the very nature of man as a creature who learns, who moves from imperfect knowledge to perfect knowledge, from potency to act. Every teacher recognizes this reality in his students, and in himself as well. The professor of chemistry brings his students by way of what they know—with balls and sticks as analogies for atoms and molecules—to a grasp of the chemical properties of things. It is not a toggle switch, but the work of many courses, a work of many years. The same applies to the life of faith. The reality of an ever-deepening understanding of faith is utterly conformed to the reality of the human being and his learning; the divine pedagogy is perfectly attuned to the reality of man.[40]

39 ST II-II.2.1.resp.
40 ST II-II.2.3.resp.

The virtue, however, must be exercised in order to be strengthened and not to wither away. In acting repeatedly, one is ever more disposed to act and with ever greater delight. In this way, the virtue becomes more and more like a second nature. The virtue makes the man and his acts good.

So far, I have stressed that faith is an act of the intellect, and so it is. But the kind of assent that is found in faith does not arise naturally in the intellect when the object is something not seen. The intellect must be moved to that assent, and it is so moved by the will. The will, in turn, is moved by grace.[41] When the faith is proclaimed, its goodness moves the will by grace, such that the will moves the intellect to assent to this truth. Yet again, a careful consideration of the intellect brings us to the will, in this case in man's supernatural life.

We can pursue the relationship of faith and the will further by examining the theological virtue of charity. Charity, which has its seat in the will, is the love of God, who is the highest and most perfect good. It is, however, a particular

41   ST II-II.2.9.resp.

species of love: it is friendship. As friendship, it is a mutual love founded upon something shared that serves as the basis of the communion of friendship. In the case of charity, this basis is divine beatitude, it is the very life of God which he gives to man so that man might participate in it and in so doing come to friendship with him.[42] The basis of friendship with God, then, is precisely God himself as the highest good, but as a good in which the human being is called to participate, and which is the object of charity. How does one relate to the object of charity, that perfect and highest good? Man cannot love what he does not know. If he does not know God as his final end, the highest good, he cannot so love him; but that is precisely how he is to love him in charity, as him in whose divine beatitude he is called to live for all eternity. How does one know this? Through faith. In this way, for Thomas faith has priority over both hope and charity, which are virtues of the will. Thomas is so precise on this point that he teaches that the first movement of the will, under grace, which moves the intellect to assent in faith is not itself charity, since charity

42   ST II-II.23.1.resp.

presupposes faith. The will cannot tend to God in the love that is charity unless the intellect has right faith concerning God.[43]

At the same time, faith needs charity. The perfection of the act of faith requires two things. First, the intellect must tend infallibly to the true; second, the intellect must be infallibly ordered to its final end—which is what charity does.[44] Thus, while charity requires faith, faith in its perfection requires charity, for with charity the will moves faith infallibly to its good, which is the true. Faith so moved is faith formed by charity and thus perfect faith.

For the same reason, charity is the form of all the virtues. As the love of the ultimate end, charity orders all the other virtues and their acts to that ultimate end. Everything is now willed insofar as it is ordered to that final end which is loved, for that final end is loved for itself, and all other things are loved insofar as they are ordered to it.[45]

43 ST II-II.4.8.ad 5m.
44 ST II-II.4.5.resp.
45 ST II-II.43.8; see also ST II-II.23.4.ad 2m: "Et ideo quia charitas habet pro objecto ultimum finem humanae vitae, scilicet beatitudinem aeternam, ideo extendit se ad actus totius humanae vitae . . ."

In addition to the theological virtues, there are the gifts of the Holy Spirit. Thomas considers the highest of the gifts, wisdom, in its relation with charity. Wisdom is a gift of the Holy Spirit in the intellect, but Thomas nonetheless associates it with charity.[46] Wisdom considers the highest causes and thus aids the Christian to judge most certainly and thereby to order all things.[47] Thus, in the gift of wisdom we find the perfection of judgment according to the highest causes, while in charity we have the infallible movement of all things in an ordering, judged by wisdom, to the good. We return yet again to the wise man, now ordering his life according to the perfecting supernatural principles of faith—which assents to the first truth—and charity, which loves and moves to the highest good under the inspiration of the gift of wisdom, which judges and orders.

There are more virtues and gifts. We have, however, considered enough to grasp the significance of Thomas's understanding of these virtues and gifts in terms of life: here we find the perfection of man in his self-moving with regard to

46   ST II-II.45.2.
47   ST II-II.45.1.

both form and end. We thus see the perfection of his rational nature. For the human being, the very perfection of his life lies in those dispositions that flow from and in turn shape his self-movement. For the Christian, this perfection occurs in the beatific vision. Yet even in this life it is already begun in the life of faith, in which the very life of man, natural and supernatural, is ever more perfectly ordered and unified under the virtues of faith and charity.

We are now in a position to appreciate Thomas the teacher all the more. In his first treatment of life in the *Summa theologiae* he skillfully explains man's place among all living things, including God. He establishes the excellence and limitations of man's self-motion on the basis of his intellectual nature. This very excellence then opens up the habituated forms of life, understood through a kind of similitude to the more basic works of life. In all of this he elucidates what is implicit in common speech. The notion of similitude in turn serves Thomas well in his study of man's supernatural life. It pertains both to the beatific vision and to the imperfect life of faith; but it also maintains the fundamental unity of the supernatural life ordered to final participation in divine life. All of this is grounded in the analysis of man whose very being is to live, but to live to the fullness of his nature, a nature fittingly graced by God so as to share in his divine and most perfect life. In these steps, we can see not only the precision of Thomas's analysis of life and faith, but also the exquisite ordering of his teaching in the *Summa theologiae* as an elucidation of that life.

III.

The Master of the Sacred Page

Let us take our theme of Master Thomas and the fullness of life one final step further. When Dr. Rosemann invited me, on behalf of the Philosophy Department, to deliver the Aquinas Lecture, I pointed out to him that he was inviting a theologian (or at least a member of a Theology Department), not a philosopher. He assured me that this was not a problem—after all, there is much philosophy in Aquinas's theology and, he said, it is not as if I was going to speak on Thomas's Scripture commentaries. Well, little did he know. I must apologize to Professor Rosemann, for that is precisely what I am going to do. Perhaps because when I arrived at the

Pontifical Institute I was still a Protestant, I became interested in what was then a largely neglected area of study: the Scripture commentaries of Aquinas. I have spent much of my scholarly life trying to figure out what Thomas is up to in those commentaries. Thomas was, after all, a master of theology, and in the thirteenth century at least, that meant that his work in the classroom consisted in commenting on Scripture. He never taught Aristotle or even his own *summae*. He taught Scripture. So I beg your indulgence and patience as I expand a bit more on this topic of Master Thomas and the fullness of life by venturing into the thicket of his commentaries on Scripture, where his work as a teacher reaches its apex.

In Thomas's article arguing for the fittingness of a creed, the first objection notes that Scripture is the rule of faith, so that there is no need for anything else. Thomas replies that the truth of faith is contained in Sacred Scripture in various ways, diffusely, and in places obscurely, such that to derive the truth of faith from Sacred Scripture requires great effort and lengthy study, which is simply not possible for many who nonetheless need to know the truth of faith. For this reason, it was necessary to gather from Scripture what needed to be presented in a summary way to all for belief.[1] If the creeds are a summary, Scripture represents the depths—and difficult depths indeed! Thomas is no naïve reader of Scripture. He knows its difficulty. He also knows its riches. Scripture is a peculiar thing that requires its own teaching. For Master Thomas it has its own proper place in the ordering of one's life to God.

Let us consider the relationship between Thomas's systematic works, such as the *summae* and the disputed questions, and his Scripture commentaries. Recently, I proposed an admittedly hokey metaphor for the relationship of the *Summa* to Scripture commentaries, drawn from the work of the biologist.[2] The *Summa*, and the speculative works generally, are like lab work: careful study of living things, principally revealed divine realities and creation as seen in the light of those realities, but under carefully controlled conditions as in a laboratory. The Scripture commentaries, on the other hand, are more like field

1   ST II-II.1.9.ad 1.
2   See J. F. Boyle, "On the Relation of St. Thomas's Commentary on Romans to the *Summa theologiae*" (2012), esp. 81–82.

work: the observation of the objects of theological inquiry in manifold living relationships one to another. Of course, this is a metaphor, and I am trying to express a matter of emphasis in these different kinds of works by Thomas. So let me try to articulate this idea more precisely.

As Cardinal Cajetan famously remarked, Thomas speaks most formally. This is a hallmark of Thomas's speculative theological works. He strives to articulate what is most proper to a thing, what is its intelligible *ratio*, which serves as the basis for its definition. This is the articulation of just what kind of a thing this thing is. It is the business of definition and distinction so dear to the scholastics, which I described at the beginning of my lecture. This is what I mean by lab work: carefully controlled intellectual study and with it some dissection, cutting the thing open and analyzing what is inside. This is Thomas on life and faith as considered above.

Thomas's Scripture commentaries are not devoid of such formal analysis, but what is there is, often enough, also found in the *Summa* or other speculative works. The Scripture commentaries disappoint if one looks for new formal analyses; such analyses are rather more presumed than articulated in the Scripture commentaries. Thomas knows that there is more to understanding reality than simply considering things most formally. In the Scripture commentaries, he is especially attentive to the relationships articulated or implied in Scripture or, perhaps better, to the manifold ways in which the realities of Christian life and revelation are related. The *summae* do indeed capture some of these relationships. They do not simply perform the discrete analysis of things, even though we do speak of the *Summa theologiae*'s "treatises." The organization of the whole is also a mark of the genius of the *Summa*, in which Thomas seeks to order the revealed truths one to another. This is simply to say, as I argue above, that the *Summa* is a work of wisdom; it is not an encyclopedia. But the *Summa* (indeed, any *summa*) cannot articulate the full causal and relational realities of what has been revealed as they are expressed in the particularity of Scripture. That is the work of the Scripture commentary, which is why I suggest that the Scripture commentary is like the biologist's field work. As the biologist in the field studies living things in their dynamic and complex relations to another, so Thomas views Sacred

Scripture as a place to study the living realities of revelation in their dynamic and complex relationships.

Some years ago I mused, in print and in passing, that the *Summa* might be a vade-mecum for the student of Scripture.[3] Too casually the modern scholar looks to the Scripture commentaries to illuminate the *Summa*. Perhaps it should be the other way around. Might not the *Summa* give its reader the foundational conceptual tools with which he is better able to undertake the serious study of Sacred Scripture? The *Summa* is, after all, intended for beginners in theology, that is, for those preparing for the careful and sustained exposition of Sacred Scripture. The reader of Thomas's commentaries who is armed with the *Summa* is a better reader of the Scripture commentaries, and ultimately a better reader of Scripture itself.

But there is something further in Thomas's purpose, which is what I attempted to capture in the metaphor of the biologist's work. Thomas is not simply interested in making sense of

---

3   See J. F. Boyle, "Thomas Aquinas and Sacred Scripture" (1995).

Scripture; or, rather, he is interested in making sense of Scripture, because he thinks it ultimately and profoundly helps him make sense of reality. Both *Summa* and Scripture commentary, in complementary and interrelated ways, illuminate reality. The mind's grasp of reality requires the careful formal work of the *Summa*, but it also requires the study of the moving and relational dimensions of that reality as presented in Scripture.

With this in mind, I would like to consider, in a limited and thoroughly inadequate way, how our topic might look in a Scripture commentary. We have done some lab work; let us take a brief moment out in the field. Specifically, I would like to consider Thomas's commentary on the Gospel according to St. John.

Thomas claims that St. John's intention in writing his Gospel is to "show the divinity of the incarnate Word."[4] This is the overarching idea, the vision, of the Gospel, and in its light, Thomas writes his commentary. Thomas is hardly the first to see this as the principal theme of St. John's

---

4   Thomas Aquinas, *Super Evangelium s. Ioannis lectura*, ed. R. Cai (1952), chap. 1, lect. 1, no. 22.

Gospel. But let us consider this idea in the context of Thomas's understanding of life. The Incarnation of the Word is one of the *per se* objects of faith—in other words, it is one of those objects of faith that are essential for bringing man in faith to eternal life. Thus, for Thomas, the Gospel according to St. John, as the beloved apostle's exposition of the divinity of Christ, functions as an exposition of that reality, which is essential to the life of faith. To study the Gospel according to St. John in faith is to bring one ever closer to that reality; it is to grow towards a more perfect life, for it is to know more perfectly in faith.

But we can take our considerations further. The very substance of my talk, life, is mentioned in St. John's words towards the end of his Gospel. Having recounted Jesus' appearance to the apostles, and specifically to the apostle Thomas, John says, "Jesus performed many other signs in the presence of his disciples which are not written in this book. These have been written so that you might believe that Jesus Christ is the Son of God and that believing you might have life in his name" (Jn 20:30–31). Thomas remarks at the beginning of this *lectio* that in these words St. John offers "the recapitulation of those things which have been said in the Gospel."[5] Apparently, then, one can consider the whole of St. John's Gospel to be about belief in Jesus Christ precisely so that one might have life. For a verse that is the recapitulation of the Gospel, the commentary itself is, perhaps, surprisingly brief. St. Thomas writes:

> Now he posits the usefulness of what he has written because it brings about faith. **These have been written so that you might believe that Jesus Christ is the Son of God and that believing you might have life in his name.** For all Scripture, both the Old and the New Testaments, is for this purpose; Ps. 39:9: "It is written of me at the head of the book"; above [Jn] 5:9: "Search the scriptures . . . it is they that bear witness to me." Again, [he posits the usefulness of what he has written] because of the fruit of life, **and that believing you may have life;** here the life of justice, which is had through

5   Ibid., chap. 20, lect. 6, divisio textus, no. 2551.

faith, Hab. 2:4: "My just man lives by faith," and in the future, the life of vision, which is had through glory; and **in his name**, namely, the name of Christ; Acts 4:12: "There is no other name under heaven given by which we must be saved."[6]

Brief, but in its way a remarkable summary of Christian existence. The usefulness of what John has written—that is to say, of the Gospel itself—is twofold: to bring about both faith and the fruit of life. The very proclamation of Christ and his teachings, found in the entirety of Sacred Scripture, serves to bring about faith. Secondly, through that faith, the Gospel bears fruit, namely, the fruit of life, which is in turn twofold. The first fruit is the life of justice, the life of the just man, which, as Thomas puts it so simply, is had through faith. This leads to the second fruit: the life of vision, which is opened to the human being in faith, is the fruit of faith, but is obtained through glory. In Thomas's brief exposition, we encounter the very sequence of supernatural life

6   Ibid., no. 2568.

that we have been considering previously: faith, the life of justice, and the life of glory. A fuller understanding of the sequence would require consideration of justice (both the virtue and the justification of the sinner) and glory as Thomas articulates them in the speculative works, much as we did with faith. Nonetheless, we can understand the essential causality of faith and life, and of the life of righteousness as it is causally ordered to the life of glory in the future. Moreover, we can see how central Christ is in this causality, as he is the final and efficient cause of supernatural life. It is in this way that Thomas understands this verse as the recapitulation of the Gospel.

How might these insights affect one's reading of Thomas's commentary? One could look to the many verses in which St. John speaks of life and consider Thomas's commentary upon them, which would bear much fruit. But there is a yet deeper way to see the centrality of life in Thomas's commentary, and that is the division of the text.

The division of the text is a remarkable scholastic technique for the interpretation and teaching of texts. The idea is simple. One begins with the intention of the author, in the light of which the commentator divides and sub-divides the text into increasingly smaller units, often down to the individual words. The author's intention provides a conceptual unity to the text and the commentary as a whole. By intention, Thomas means what the author set himself to accomplish, that is, the final cause of the work.[7] Because the division begins with the whole and then continues through progressive subdivisions, every verse stands in an articulated relation not only with the whole, but ultimately with every other part, division, and verse of the text.[8] In commenting on St. John's Gospel, Thomas provides such a division of the text. (See appendix.)

As noted already, St. John's intention, according to Thomas, is to "show the divinity of the incarnate Word"; this is the principal theme in

---

7   One ought not to confuse Thomas's understanding of intention with the modern understanding of it as "what the author means." See J. F. Boyle, "Authorial Intention and the *divisio textus*" (2005).

8   See J. F. Boyle, "The Theological Character of the Scholastic 'Division of the Text' with Particular Reference to the Commentaries of St. Thomas Aquinas" (2003).

light of which Thomas divides the text. He first divides the Gospel into two parts: in the first, St. John presents the divinity of Christ (chap. 1), and in the second he manifests that divinity through those things Christ did in the flesh (chaps. 2–21). These two parts are in turn further divided.

In the division of the first chapter, which treats the divinity of Christ, Thomas distinguishes the consideration of the being of the Word with regard to its divine nature (vv. 1–2) and the consideration of the operation of the Word (vv. 3–4). With regard to the operation of the Word, Thomas says the Word shows his power with regard to all things that come into being ("all things were made through Him"), and specifically with regard to man ("and the life was the light of men"). What specifically pertains to man as the most perfect degree of life among inferior creatures is his relation to the light. Thomas interprets light here with regard to the Word in two different ways.[9] One can take the Word in

9 For what follows, see Thomas Aquinas, *Super Evangelium s. Ioannis lectura*, ed. R. Cai (1952), chap. 1, lectio 3, nos. 95–104. Multiple literal interpretations of a given passage of Scripture are common in Thomas, who regards them as in principle

relation to natural knowledge, in which the Word as light is the source of natural cognition because it is truth itself. In this light, man not only knows particular true things but rather the very notion (*ratio*) of truth. Appealing to the characteristics of natural light, Thomas claims that this light is both manifestable and manifesting. The truth itself is manifestable to the human intellect by man's very nature, but it also manifests particular truths.

Thomas goes still further, again following the nature of physical light and physical sight, to assert that man not only knows the divine light as an object, but that, in the higher part of his soul, he participates in that light which is the Word, for such participation makes possible the very intellection by which he knows the truth. This especially matters to man as the most perfect of inferior creatures because, among those creatures, the human being is the one that most perfectly moves itself. Although other living things move themselves by some intrinsic principle, only man can move himself freely since his action is

possible and sound. See J. F. Boyle, "Authorial Intention and the *divisio textus*" (2005).

always with regard to opposites and therefore not determined. In his relationship to the truth itself he is able to move himself freely and order his life rightly.

In all of this, Thomas speaks of the light of natural knowledge, which is available to all human beings. What he claims here is that this light is the divine Word, who is the second person of the Trinity.

The second way in which Thomas reads "and the life was the light of men" is that the Word assumed flesh so that he might illumine all men through grace and truth. This interpretation views light according to the order of grace, bestowed through the Incarnation of the Word. Thomas quotes words of Christ that occur later on in John's Gospel: "For this I was born and for this I came, that I might give testimony to the truth," and "As long as I am in the world, I am the light of the world" (Jn 18:37 and 9:5). Both of these quotations figure in the part of the division of the text which pertains to Christ's teaching as an effect of grace, a grace that is a benefit bestowed on those regenerated into new life. Thomas concludes his comments as follows:

> Fittingly, he joins light and life, saying **and the life was the light of men**, that he might show these two things, namely light and life, came to us through Christ: indeed, life through participation in grace, as below [Jn 5:17]: "Grace and truth is accomplished through Jesus Christ"; and light through knowledge of truth and wisdom.[10]

Christ is the new life of man, a life of participation in the grace of Christ, who is God himself. This life is grace as specified in the light that is knowledge and truth, which give order and end to human life. They are here tied to the incarnate Word, through whom both the imperfect life of faith and the perfect life of glory are brought about.

In these two interpretations, we find Thomas considering light with regard to both man's natural and supernatural life. The Word stands as the efficient, formal (by way of participation), and final cause of man's life as an intellectual being,

10   Thomas Aquinas, *Super Evangelium s. Ioannis lectura*, ed. R. Cai (1952), chap. 1, lect. 3, no. 104.

acting both naturally and supernaturally. We see here Thomas's understanding of life, and specifically human life, as being inextricably linked to the second person of the Trinity and the redemptive Incarnation. It is an exquisite example of how grace perfects nature in the teaching of Thomas.

Let us return to the second part of the division of the text, which treats the manifestation of Christ's divinity through what he did. This portion of the text is subdivided into two parts, devoted respectively to the manner in which Christ manifests his divinity while living in the world (chaps. 2–11), and to the way in which Christ manifests his divinity in his death (chaps. 12–21). The manifestation of Christ's divinity during his life in the world is divided into two parts: manifesting his dominion over nature (chap. 2), and manifesting the effects of grace (chaps. 3–11). These effects include spiritual regeneration (chaps. 3–4), and spiritual goods conferred upon those divinely regenerated (chaps. 5–11). These spiritual goods are, in turn, threefold: spiritual life (chap. 5), spiritual food (chap. 6), and spiritual teaching (chaps. 7–11). Each of these sections is further divided and subdivided, but we need not follow the division any further.

Notice just how prominently life figures in the division of the text. Within the context of Christ's manifestation of his divinity during his life in this world we have, beginning at chapter 3, a treatment of the effects of grace, but these effects are cast in the context of spiritual regeneration, that is to say, new life. Chapters 3 and 4, covering as they do the conversations with Nicodemus (on being born again) and with the Samaritan woman at the well (about the water which he will give and which gushes to eternal life), are directly about the spiritual regeneration, the spiritual life, that Christ grants. Then Thomas turns to the benefits bestowed on those to whom he has given new life: the new life itself is the subject matter of chapter 5 (on the healing of the paralytic at the pool of Bethesda, which signifies baptism); the spiritual food is treated in chapter 6 (with the feeding of the 5000 and the bread-of-life discourse, which foreshadow the Eucharist); and the spiritual teaching encompasses chapters 7 to 11 on Jesus' two trips to Jerusalem, before his final and triumphant entry leading up to his passion (in chapter 12). Even with this broad consideration of the division of the text, we can see that Thomas is putting significant elements in relation with each other: new life, its source in baptism, its refreshment in the Eucharist, and its substantive foundation in the teachings of Christ, which constitute the objects of faith.[11]

Thomas is one of the great masters of the division of the text, and we see it in his commentary on John. To say that the principal intention of St. John in his Gospel is to demonstrate the divinity of Christ is to say that his intention is to show the principal object of faith, God himself. But it is God in the mystery of the Incarnation who is proper to the Catholic faith. Moreover, the division brings out the centrality of life in the

11   The clear integration of the sacraments into the consideration of life in the commentary on St. John's Gospel reminds us of yet another analogical use of life in Thomas's work. He is the first to articulate fully the analogy from physical life to spiritual life ordered according to the sacraments, by which one is born into spiritual life though baptism, nourished by the Eucharist, healed by penance, etc. To see the importance of natural life for the development of Thomas's thinking on the sacrament of extreme unction, see J. F. Boyle, "St. Thomas Aquinas on the Anointing of the Sick (Extreme Unction)" (2009).

Gospel in relation to the mystery of Christ's divinity. And the division does still more: it situates life in relation to many other essential elements of the Gospel. It turns out, then, that the discussion of faith in the *Summa theologiae* is just the beginning. We could, of course—indeed, a careful study of Thomas's commentary would require this—return to the systematic works to examine the sacraments, for example, so as to bring out the fuller implications of the yoking of Christ's divinity, life, and the sacraments. What we can already see, even without such a study— and this is what I wish to stress here—is the way in which the division of the text lays bare the landscape of the Gospel. It is a kind of topographical map in which the many elements may be seen in relation to a whole. Precisely for this reason, if one wishes to consider the theme of life in Thomas's commentary, one cannot simply look to the passages that mention life; one must look to the whole and see the integral unity of the parts: "These have been written so that you might believe that Jesus Christ is the Son of God and that believing you might have life in his name"—this is indeed a recapitulation of the whole of the Gospel.

We get a glimpse of something symphonic, or perhaps even better fugal, in Master Thomas's commentary. Everything about Christ can be seen in the context of life: who he is, what he does, what he teachers. Everything is now in play. Christ is the divine wisdom who has ordered all things. That wisdom has come to teach, to give life. The central place of Christ the teacher in the commentary on St. John's Gospel reminds us that for Thomas, Christ is the real teacher; Thomas's work is in the service of another greater master. The greater master is of the most excellent dignity, for he impresses his teaching upon the very hearts of his hearers. His teaching itself is of such surpassing excellence that it cannot be comprehended in words. For these reasons Christ himself never committed his teachings to writing. It is fitting, therefore, that his teachings should come to be known through others who teach both verbally and in writing. Thomas quotes Proverbs, speaking about wisdom, to the effect that "she sent out her handmaids to call to the tower" (Prov 9:3).[12] Thomas

12 I draw here on ST III.42.4.resp. K. White, "Aquinas on Oral Teaching" (2007), illuminates Thomas's

must have seen himself as one of wisdom's hand-maids.

At the beginning of this lecture, I remarked how much Thomas's thought and work do not represent a system. They are systematic but possess an openness, even an incompleteness, that is arresting. Perhaps we can see at least one reason why. Thomas does not consider his teaching to be his own. He seeks merely to make another's teachings better understood. His task is to make the greatest teacher understood, but this task, in its completeness, ultimately and always eludes the human intellect.

On the feast of St. Nicholas, December 6th, 1273, after celebrating Mass early in the morning, St. Thomas did not resume his work. Although he would live for another three months, he would not teach or write again. Thomas told his faithful confrere and socius, Brother Reginald, "All that I have written seems to me straw compared to those things which I have seen and which have been revealed to me." We do not know what the master saw that morn-

comparison of Christ to Socrates on this point of oral versus written teaching.

ing at Mass such that he would not teach again. Religious experience was hardly new to him;[13] but this one, it seems, was different. He says he saw something. I cannot help but think that he was given to see that beatific vision, that fullness of life, to which he had so tirelessly ordered his own earthly life; he saw, however fleetingly, that eternal life which he had so labored, as a good master, to understand himself and in turn make known to his students. Compared to life at its fullness, what he wrote was indeed so much straw. For some of us still here and not so graced, we are grateful for the straw.

13 See J. Goering, "The Miracles and Visions of Thomas Aquinas" (2002).

Appendix

St. Thomas Aquinas's Division of the Gospel according to St. John[1]

The Gospel according to St. John principally intends to show the divinity of the incarnate Word.

I. John sets forth the divinity of Christ (chap. 1);
    A. he sets forth the divinity of Christ (1.1–1.13);

---

1   This division is taken from Thomas Aquinas, *Super Evangelium s. Ioannis lectura*, ed. R. Cai (1952); of course the division continues well into each chapter down to the verse.

1. he sets forth the divinity of Christ (1.1–1.5);
   a. concerning the being of the Word with regard to divine nature (1.1–1.2);
   b. concerning the power or operation of the Word (1.3–1.5);
      i. his power with regard to all things which come into being (1.3–1.4a);
      ii. his power specifically with regard to men (1.4b–1.5);
2. he sets forth the incarnation of the Word (1.6–1.13);

B. he sets forth the manner in which Christ's divinity is made known (1.14–1.51).

II. He manifests the divinity of Christ by what he did in the flesh (2.1–21.25);
   A. how Christ manifests his divinity in those things he did while living in the world (2.1–11.57)
      1. in his dominion over nature (chap. 2);
      2. in the effects of grace (3.1–11.57);

a. spiritual regeneration
(3.1–4.54);
b. benefits conferred on those
regenerated (5.1–11.57);
    i. spiritual life (chap. 5);
    ii. spiritual food (chap. 6);
    iii. spiritual teaching
      (7.1–11.57);
      aa. its origin (chap. 7);
      bb. its power
        (8.1–11.57);
B. how Christ showed his divinity in his
death (12.1–21.25);
  1. Christ's passion and death
  (12.1–19.42);
    a. causes and occasion of Christ's
    death (chap. 12);
    b. preparation of the disciples
    (13.1–17.26);
      i. how he informed them by
        example (chap. 13);
      ii. how he comforted them in
        word (14.1–16.33);
      iii. how he strengthened
        them by prayer (chap. 17);

    c. passion and death
      (18.1–19.42);
         i. passion at the hands of the
           Jews (chap. 18);
        ii. passion at the hands of the
           Gentiles (chap. 19);
2. the resurrection (20.1–21.25);
    a. manifest to the women
      (20.1–20.18);
    b. manifest to the disciples
      (20.18–21.25).

Bibliography

Works by
St. Thomas Aquinas

In octo libros Physicorum Aristotelis expositio, ed. P. M. Maggiòlo (Turin: Marietti, 1965).

Lectura romana in primum Sententiarum Petri Lombardi, ed. Leonard E. Boyle, O.P. and John F. Boyle (Toronto: Pontifical Institute of Mediaeval Studies, 2006).

Scriptum super libros Sententiarum, ed. P. Mandonnet, O.P., volume 1 (Paris: Lethielleux, 1929).

Summa contra gentiles, in *Opera omnia*, cura et studio Fratrum Praedicatorum [Leonine Commission], vols. 13–15 (Rome: Typis Riccardi Garroni, 1918–1930).

Summa theologiae. Cura et studio Instituti Studiorum Medievalium Ottaviensis (Ottawa: Commissio Piana, 1953), 5 vols.

Super Evangelium S. Ioannis lectura, ed. R. Cai (Turin: Marietti, 1952).

Super primam epistolam ad Corinthios lectura, in *Super epistolas S. Pauli lectura,* ed. R. Cai, 8th ed. (Turin: Marietti, 1953), vol. 1, 231–435.

Further Reading

Boyle, John F., "Is the *tertia pars* of the *Summa theologiae* misplaced?" *Proceedings of the PMR Conference* 18 (1993–1994): 103–09.

———, "Thomas Aquinas and Sacred Scripture," *Pro Ecclesia* 4 (1995): 92–104.

———, "St. Thomas Aquinas and the Analogy of *potentia generandi,*" *The Thomist* 64 (2000): 581–92.

———, "The Theological Character of the Scholastic 'Division of the Text' with Particular Reference to the Commentaries of St. Thomas Aquinas," in *With Reverence for the Word: Medieval Scriptural Exegesis in*

Judaism, Christianity and Islam, ed. Jane McAuliffe, Barry Walfish, and Joseph Goering (Oxford: Oxford University Press, 2003), 276–83.

———, "Authorial Intention and the *divisio textus*," in *Reading John with St. Thomas Aquinas: Theological Exegesis and Speculative Theology*, ed. Michael Dauphinais and Matthew Levering (Washington, D.C.: The Catholic University of America Press, 2005), 3–8.

———, "The Analogy of 'Homo' and 'Deus' in St. Thomas Aquinas's *Lectura romana*," *Nova et Vetera* 6 (2008): 663–7.

———, "St. Thomas Aquinas on the Anointing of the Sick (Extreme Unction)," in *Rediscovering Aquinas and the Sacraments: Studies in Sacramental Theology*, ed. Matthew Levering and Michael Dauphinais (Chicago: Hillenbrand Books, 2009), 76–84.

———, "Thomas Aquinas and His *Lectura romana in primum Sententiarum Petri Lombardi*," in *Mediaeval Commentaries on the Sentences of Peter Lombard*, vol. 2, ed. Philipp W. Rosemann (Leiden: Brill, 2010), 149–73.

————, "Aquinas' Lost *Roman Commentary*: An Historical Detective Story," in *Thomas Aquinas—Teacher and Scholar: The Aquinas Lectures at Maynooth*, vol. 2: *2002–2010*, ed. James McEvoy, Michael Dunne, and Julia Hynes (Dublin: Four Courts Press, 2012), 71–84.

————, "On the Relation of St. Thomas's Commentary on Romans to the *Summa theologiae*," in *Reading Romans with St. Thomas Aquinas*, ed. Matthew Levering and Michael Dauphinais (Washington, D.C.: The Catholic University of America Press, 2012), 75–82.

Boyle, Leonard E., O.P., *The Setting of the "Summa theologiae" of Saint Thomas* (Toronto: Pontifical Institute of Mediaeval Studies, 1982), repr. with revisions in Leonard E. Boyle, O.P., *Facing History: A Different Thomas Aquinas* (Louvain-la-Neuve: Fédération internationale des instituts d'études médiévales, 2000), 65–91.

Goering, Joseph, "The Miracles and Visions of Thomas Aquinas," in *Mystics, Visions, and Miracles*, ed. Joseph Goering, Francesco

Guardiani, and Giulio Silano (Ottawa: Legas, 2002), 127–39.

Long, Steven A., *Natura pura: On the Recovery of Nature in the Doctrine of Grace* (New York: Fordham University Press, 2010).

———, *Analogia entis: On the Analogy of Being, Metaphysics, and the Act of Faith* (Notre Dame: University of Notre Dame Press, 2011).

Weisheipl, James A., O.P., "The Meaning of *Sacra Doctrina* in *Summa Theologiae* I, q. 1," *The Thomist* 38 (1974): 49–80.

White, Kevin, "Aquinas on Oral Teaching," *The Thomist* 71 (2007): 505–28.